Ghost Hunting: A Beginner's Guide to Investigating the Dead

GHOST HUNTING

BEGINNERS GUIDE
TO INVESTIGATING THE DEAD

WRITTEN BY
RANDALL CROPP

OVERVIEW

CHAPTER ONE – WHAT ARE GHOSTS AND WHY DO WE HUNT THEM?

HERE WE WILL DISCUSS THE ORIGINS OF GHOSTS AND THEIR PLACE IN OUR GLOBAL HISTORY.

CHAPTER TWO – WHAT TOOLS WILL I NEED?

FROM EVP DETECTORS TO SPIRIT BOXES, EVERYTHING YOU NEED TO COMPLETE YOUR INVESTIGATION.

CHAPTER THREE – MY FAVORITE GHOST HUNTING TECHNIQUES.

THERE'S MORE TO GHOST HUNTING THAN SITTING IN THE DARK. THESE ARE MY TRIED AND TRUE METHODS OF PURSUING THE DEAD.

CHAPTER FOUR – PUTTING TOGETHER YOUR GHOST HUNTING TEAM.

WHY GO ALONE WHEN YOU CAN HAVE A TEAM? HERE ARE THE METHODS I UTILIZED WHEN PUTTING TOGETHER MY ROSTER OF FELLOW INVESTIGATORS.

CHAPTER FIVE – CONDUCTING YOUR FIRST GHOST HUNT

YOUR FIRST HUNT IS A **HUGE** DEAL. GET THE MOST OUT OF YOUR INVESTIGATION BY FOLLOWING MY ADVICE AND AVOIDING MY MISTAKES.

INTRODUCTION

Hi there!

Thank you for downloading my e-book, 'Ghost Hunting: A Beginner's Guide to Investigating the dead'.

The act of ghost hunting, or ghost investigating, has drawn equal parts ire and amazement over the years that the craft has been popularized. Whether you come to me by way of your fascination with paranormal television shows (*Ghost Adventures, Ghost Hunters, Paranormal Lockdown*) or your own experiences is irrespective. You are here because you are fascinated by the dead and you want to know how to communicate with them.

I can help you out.

I began my search for the paranormal with a cynical abandon. A friend had invited me to attend a ghost investigation with him at the Schiller Piano Factory in Oregon, IL -- my home town. I came for a laugh and left with a new perspective on life. It sounds melodramatic, and perhaps it is, but that was the truth. I found something in the darkness of our hunt, and I captured it with my audio recorder, and ever since then my life has been different.

It used to be that I was afraid of the dark but now I am fascinated by what I may find within it.

So, if you share this same fascination then you might be interested in learning how to investigate on your own or with another team. I have compiled a long list of helpful techniques and educational documents for your perusal. By reading this book you should find yourself prepared, equipped, and educated on what it takes to pursue the paranormal world.

So without much further deliberation let's begin the process. Your life is going to be changing very shortly.

PREFACE

For as long as humans have been alive we have been fascinated by death. The mere idea of life and death should be enough to shake you to your core — whatever *you* actually are. Are you a spirit that is trapped in a physical shell sent here by some God up above? Are you merely a conception of humanity, playing out your role in someone else's dream? These questions are unanswerable. We don't know what life really is. We also don't really understand death.

Death.

The word is so short, so simple, and so finite. I assume that death is what brought you to my book. You are curious about what happens *after*. After life. The afterlife. You want to find out how you can communicate with ghosts, with spirits, with whatever *they* are. Maybe you've seen the television shows that showcase 'ghost hunters' going from haunted building to haunted building. Maybe you've had your own personal experience with something beyond the grave. Maybe you think that this is all a joke and you are just here for a laugh.

In a way it doesn't matter what you think. We are here to talk about communing with the dead, whatever *death* may mean to you. I've been hunting ghosts for years and what's more: I've been finding them. I was once a skeptic of all things dealing with ghosts, religion and the paranormal. I once teetered on the edge of complete apathy and that apathy very nearly killed me. Then I talked to someone beyond the grave. I communicated with someone on the Other Side, whatever that may mean. As a result my life has changed. I've found purpose. I've found a question to cling to: What does death actually mean? Death certainly doesn't mean the end of us, I now know that for a fact.

Today I am going to teach you the fundamentals of hunting ghosts, of communicating with the dead. I'm going to walk you through my techniques and impart on you some of the wisdom I've found during my experiences. This book is meant to be used as another tool in your ghost hunting toolbox. You don't need to read it from cover to cover. Pick through and find the information that you need.

Happy hunting.

CHAPTER ONE

WHAT ARE GHOSTS AND WHY DO WE HUNT THEM?

If you were to ask a dozen different paranormal enthusiasts this question, you would likely get a dozen different answers. Speaking on the subject of ghosts requires you to open up your mind just a little bit and to allow speculation to run wild. We'll first delve into the accepted definition of ghosts before moving on with my own perspective.

GHOST - NOUN - DEFINITION

An apparition of a dead person that is believed to appear or become manifest to the living, typically as a nebulous image.

There you have it in layman's terms. A ghost is just a representation of a once living being. Simple, right? This dictionary definition may wrap things up with a bow but it does nothing to actually explain to us what a spirit actually is. Let's put our dictionary away. Here is my perspective which has been learned and honed through countless ghost hunting expeditions.

Your Shell, Your Spirit.

Take a moment to look at yourself. Do you see your body, your flesh? Everything that comprises your physical being is simply a shell. What *you are* is the spark underneath. You are the 'I' in your head. You are the running monologue that never stops. *You* are an ego, intellect, mind and soul all wrapped up into one Being. When you pass on, that is to say, when your physical body ceases to thrive, it is this collection of concepts that continues to exist.

In physics there is the **law of conservation of energy** that insists that energy cannot be destroyed nor created — it simply moves from container to container. There is a lot of scientific jargon that goes behind this concept but you don't need to know it all right now. Our soul, whatever *we* are, is comprised of energy. When our bodily shell ceases to be, our spirit is released and our energy continues on.

When I sit inside of an old hospital and I bust out my EVP monitor I am communicating with a person as represented by their spiritual energy. This is the same person that once existed within a fleshly shell only now they are made free of their physical manifestation. I don't blame you if you are already tuning me out. This is a tough concept to swallow and it is even harder to balance against the various religions in the world. I don't think the belief in ghosts runs afoul of most religion but that is another topic for another day.

Dealing in Demons.

Maybe you are on board with my concept of spiritual energy but that could leave you wondering about demons and poltergeists. If you've spent even a minute of your time dealing in the paranormal then you've no doubt read about these spiritual troublemakers. How do we weigh the concept of our personal spiritual energy against something that may never have been human at all?

The concept of demonic entities can be traced back all the way to ancient Greek mythology though the status of the word has changed over time. Demons, as we know them, have been made more popular by Christian religion and Hollywood crafted entertainment. Still, the source is neither here nor there. We are here to discuss what a demon actually is.

The most commonly accepted idea of a demon is thus: an evil spirit that seeks to do you harm.

Again, that is a dictionary type definition that wraps the word up with a neat little bow. However, there is so much more going on here than what we can explain with simple words.

In my personal experience, which has thankfully been rather limited in this regard, demons are spirits that represent our most basic, negative desires. They are spirits that want to do damage in any way that they can. This could manifest itself in sowing discord amongst friends, promoting violence, or even in actual out and out possession. The movies get a lot wrong when dealing with the paranormal, but the concept of possession is as real as it is scary.

We can turn to the Bible for what we believe is an accurate depiction of what a demon actually is:

MATTHEW 12:43, KING JAMES VERSION

When the unclean spirit is gone out of a man, he walketh through dry places, seeking rest, and findeth none.

If you were to take the Bible seriously in this regard then you would have to conclude that demons were once human. From this passage we can infer that demons are the spirits of humans who were forced from their body due to their own evil doings. The goal of these demonic entities is now to find a new body to inhabit. Or, at the very least, to render their angst upon the living so as to make someone else's physical life as miserable as their's once was. Demons lust after the living. They want to take your energy. They want to inhabit your body. They want to harm you. If this doesn't scare you then you aren't ready to continue on.

Hunting Ghosts: A Noble Pursuit.

If you are accepting of my words then you now understand what spirits are or, more accurately, what they likely could be. Do you accept these words? Do you still want to pursue communing with the dead? We thought so. Let's talk about why you should and *shouldn't* ghost hunt.

Some people seek out the spiritual world because they want to find a lost loved one. They want to once more connect with a spirit that they knew in his or her physical form. We do not suggest pursuing ghost hunting if this is why you've come to us. When you pursue ghosts you are opening yourself up to them. Someone who is emotionally raw, seeking closure, opens up their soul to demonic entities and thus they put themselves at risk. In all things dangerous we counsel caution. Shrug yourself free of this concept and find closure in other ways.

I suggest pursuing the world of ghost hunting for a far more noble reason: knowledge. There is no pursuit more pure than that of knowledge and I firmly believe that we owe it to ourselves to understand as much as possible of the world around us. By embracing the concepts of spirits, by pursuing them with the techniques you are about to learn, you can round out your understanding of what life actually **is**. Could there be any reason more profound?

A Final Note.

You've made it through my ramblings and are close to embarking on your quest. Before you go I want to take a moment to warn you, to let you pause and really reflect. The pursuit of ghosts is a life changing endeavor. The first time I heard a voice come through my audio recorder ... I was stunned. I had been born and raised a skeptic. I challenged the very notion of the spirit. I was a cynical being who was floating through life and taking everything at face value. For most of my life the world had been a puddle: all shallow, all surface, all superficial. Then the voice came through and my spark was ignited. Since then I've spent nights in some of the most haunted places around. I've felt things. I've seen things. I've had conversations with beings in another realm, another phase of their existence.

I'm not the same man that I was and you won't be either. You can't dip into the Other Side without taking it home with you. This is a scary thought but it is also invigorating, enlightening and evolutionary.

Your life is about to change. Embrace it.

CHAPTER TWO

WHAT TOOLS WILL I NEED?

If you've made it this far then I know you are serious about pursuing the other side and that is why I'm about to let you sift through my tired and true, battle tested ghost hunting techniques. Like anything in life you will need to prepare at ghost hunting in order to succeed. This means that you will need to learn techniques, purchase equipment, and hone your ghost hunting mindset. Let's begin with the basics.

Ghost Hunting Toolbox.

One of my favorite paranormal television shows is called *Ghost Adventures*. While you may have opinions as to the veracity of the show, you can't deny how well prepared the crew is when they go into each investigation. What makes this crew so revolutionary is that they are constantly pushing the envelope in regards to ghost hunting technology. They always have a new device on hand. Most of these devices are garbage but a few of them work well. We believe that every investigation should begin by first assembling a well prepared toolbox. Let's take a look at my toolbox.

1. Digital Audio Recorder

The first piece of gear that you need to add to your toolbox is simple and affordable: a digital audio recording device. There is no tool more important or more profound than this piece of tech. For reasons that we can't quite comprehend, ghosts tend to communicate through these devices in the form of **EVPs**. An **EVP** is simply the acronym for **electric voice phenomena**. During an EVP session you will record yourself asking questions to a haunted room. When you play back your recording, if you are lucky, you will hear a voice answering you. You can find a recorder on Amazon for under $30. Bring a couple of these recording devices with you when you go to investigate.

Personal Experience - My digital audio recorder is the single most important piece of equipment that I own. Before filming an episode of *Project Paranormal* one of my photographers set up their audio recorder while they prepped their cameras. On the recorder I heard my camera woman say, "Sorry for all of the noise" as she rifled through her bags. Immediately after, clear as day, a woman's voice followed by saying, "Be quiet!" She was the only female in the building.

2. Digital Camcorder

The most expensive purchase you'll need to make when you begin your ghost hunting career is your camera. We suggest getting a camcorder that can record in Infrared, Ultraviolet, or Full Spectrum. Being able to record while the lights are out is of the utmost necessity. We'll get into the why's later — for now just trust us on this. Again, head to Amazon or your local electronics store to look for options that fit your budget. I've had impeccable success the **Bell & Howell** line of IR camcorders and they typically will run you under $200.

Personal Experience - I was investigating the third floor, an attic, of a building for an episode of *Project Paranormal*. We set up multiple cameras at once during our

EVP sessions. Our 'B' Cam caught an orb flying through the air and into our 'A' Cam. The 'A' Cam's battery died minutes later despite being fully charged.

3. EMF Detector

Our theory is that ghosts are actually just the energy representations of our spirit. It stands to reason that an EMF Detector will go a long way toward actually detecting spirits. EMF Detectors can be expensive when you go for higher end brands but the uptick in price is worth it. Imagine navigating through life looking for something that cannot be seen. Now, imagine that an EMF Detector is a radar that allows you to find what you are looking for. These are invaluable tools. An EMF detector shouldn't be your primary investigative tool but it makes a fine companion piece. Just be aware of false readings.

Personal Experience - I was working my way through the Schiller Piano Factory in Oregon, IL during an overnight investigation. The building was bereft of energy sensitive enough to register on our detector. We had been there for hours without picking up a single trace on our EMF detector. Suddenly, as we were walking, our EMF detector starts to rapidly beep. We immediately sat down for an EVP session. We ended up capturing voices right then and there after having spent the bulk of the night without activity.

4. Spirit Box Research Device

Ghost Adventures singlehandedly inspired an entire generation of paranormal researchers when they brought on the Spirit Box Research Device. I use the SB7, which is an older model, and have found it to be immensely helpful on investigations. A Spirit

Box is essentially a broken radio that quickly scans through either AM or FM frequencies on a radio. When it is scanning at the proper speed you will hear nothing but white noise. How is this helpful? It is my belief that the Spirit Box opens up a pathway for a spirit to communicate. When you turn on your Spirit Box you should start asking questions. If there is spirit activity in the room with you then you will hear a voice come *through* the white noise. If this is an intelligent spirit then it should respond to your questions.

Personal Experience - I was doing an investigation at the famous Ashmore Estates in Ashmore, IL. My partner and I were sitting in what once had been a private kitchen for women and children. We had been sweeping with our Spirit Box for about five or six minutes while asking questions. Nothing had come through. Finally I decided to ask the room, "Are you afraid that two men are in your kitchen?" Half a heartbeat later the Spirit Box spoke for the first time by saying, "No". The voice was as clear as day and I still get goosebumps thinking about it. That room turned into a hot spot of spiritual energy for us.

5. Audio Editing Software

If you plan to be in this field then you are going to need the tools with which to properly analyze your findings. We highly suggest downloading the free software **Audacity** in order to enhance your audio recordings. Audacity is a simple program that will allow you to clean up your audio files and make more prominent any of the voices that you capture.

Personal Experience - While some spirits seem to talk directly into our audio recorders, others will barely register at all. Using Audacity I am able to cut out as much noise as possible while boosting the frequency that our spirit is registering on.

These are the tools that I make sure to have on my person at all times. I also suggest grabbing onto a nice flashlight, spare batteries for all of your devices, and a breathing mask if you are planning on investigating condemned buildings. No paranormal evidence is worth damaging your respiratory system.

A Final Note.

When I first dive into hobbies, paranormal or otherwise, it is usually my first instinct to spend as much time and money as possible in order to prepare myself. Sometimes this quirk allows me to excel at my tasks and other times it prevents me from ever getting started. Be aware of your needs and avoid the consuming desire to over prepare. At the end of the day all you need is an audio recorder, a location with spiritual activity, and your own voice. Outside of the audio recorder my other suggestions are merely that — suggestions.

CHAPTER THREE

MY FAVORITE GHOST HUNTING TECHNIQUES.

Hunting for ghosts is sort of like painting piece of art. You can get by just knowing the broad strokes of the field but if you learn all of the little details then your work will truly excel. We are going to discuss a few different ghost hunting techniques that you can employ during your next investigation. I have used all of the techniques listed below to varying levels of success. As you'll come to learn, trying *something* is better than nothing. You never know *what* will trigger a response from the Other Side. Without further ado...

The Essentials.

1. The Burst Session - Catching EVPs is equal parts fascinating and infuriating. Often times you won't know you captured *anything* until you get home to review the audio files. Burst Sessions are great ways to try and capture something *on the spot*. For a Burst Session to work you must find a place that seems to be giving off some sort of energy. Pay attention to your body and your EMF detectors. Spirits can manifest themselves by taking your energy, thus making you feel fatigued or dizzy — even cold. If you get one of these signals then immediately fire up your digital recorder. Reel off about 60 seconds of questions, pausing long enough between each question. Then play back the recording you just took. Have headphones with you to listen closely. You might capture an EVP that leads your investigation in a new direction.

2. Solo Sessions - Imagine that you are a spirit, I know it's tough, minding your own business in the building that you call home. Suddenly five or six people come tromping into your room while armed to the teeth with cameras, recording devices, Spirit Boxes and who knows what else. You might want to hide, right? Solo sessions can be fantastic ways to draw out shy spirits. Send in an investigator, or go yourself, to a room completely alone. Conduct your EVP or Spirit Box session without any other investigator around. Sometimes the most thrilling, and chilling, evidence can be captured this way.

3. Trigger Objects - The last essential technique you need to know involves bringing a prop to your investigation. If I were doing an investigation in an old VFW, for example, I would consider bringing in parts of a soldier's uniform. Really, anything from the spirit's potential era could be useful. Your goal here is to instigate an emotional response from the spirit, thus prompting them to come out and show themselves to you in some way.

4. Your Body - Most importantly you are going to want to use your body as an instrument for your investigations. You will recognize the presence of a spirit far quicker than your devices. I've been in rooms where I've felt the temperature drop. My arms have prickled up with goosebumps. At the same time that this is happening I am capturing voices through my monitor — and I never would have known if I hadn't been paying attention. One of my most notable experiences came in an old kitchen at the Ashmore Estates. I had been doing a Spirit Box session when my partner, Christopher, kept seeing orbs in his IR monitor. At the same time that these orbs were manifesting I had begun to feel dizzy and weak. So I paused the Spirit Box and went over to him.

While we were talking, distracted, a voice started speaking in the audio recorder we had left across the room. "I'm Sorry" it said to us. I'll never know what the spirit meant but I still get chills thinking of it.

Other Techniques.

1. Provocation - This is probably going to be the most controversial inclusion on our list but we feel like it needs to be added. The act of provocation requires you to bring an angry and intense attitude to your EVP sessions. You are essentially challenging the spirit to do something, hoping that their anger will pay dividends. Embrace this technique cautiously because sometimes you won't like the evidence that you receive.

2. Night Photography - If you have a camera that is equipped with an IR light or even just a flash setting then you might want to try this technique out. Have your photographer lead the way through the halls of your building. They will take flash photographs in front of you, hoping to capture something manifesting itself in the darkness. Some wild evidence can be captured this way.

3. Thermometer - This technique can be used in conjunction with all of the other options on our list. Basically it is commonly accepted that manifesting spirits will leave a cold spot in their wake. Having a digital thermometer with a laser measuring device can help you to find specific cold spots and monitor them. We've been in buildings where the ambient temperature will sit around 70 degrees before suddenly plummeting in the wake of a spirit manifesting itself. I've sat there, stunned, while watching my thermometer drop by anywhere from 5 to 10 degrees. It's an alarming experience but one that is well worth documenting.

4. Rituals - There is a part of me that is intrinsically fascinated by the concept of utilizing ancient rituals. However, as I've said over and over again — there are some doors that are better left closed. While utilizing rituals pulled from ancient texts or, well, the internet may sound appealing, it isn't worth it. As experienced as we all my be, we aren't *that* experienced. Leave rituals to the Church and stick to the basic techniques that we've outlined above. You'll be better off for it.

A Final Note.

There are numerous other techniques that I chose not to touch on in this section of the book. I'm firmly against employing anything relating to the occult. I don't believe in utilizing psychics, Oujia Boards, rituals or anything else of the like. Other folks will swear by this but it just isn't for me and as such I won't suggest it to you.

Chapter Four

Putting together your ghost hunting team.

You can spend your entire paranormal investigating life on your own. You don't ever need to work with another person in order to capture spectacular evidence. With that being said we would be remiss if we didn't suggest putting together a team. Working with a group of individuals that share your passionate pursuit for the paranormal can enhance your own findings while creating an experience worth bonding over. Still, you need to be careful with those that you choose to team up with. Let's talk about establishing your own ghost hunting team.

1. Look Local.

When it comes time to pull together a ghost hunting team you are going to want to search for people that are in your area. While this may sound difficult, especially if you live in the rural Midwest, never fear. Paranormal enthusiasts are everywhere and all it takes is a few of the right inquiries to find them. We suggest heading to websites like Facebook or Craigslist in order to look for local ghost hunting teams. There are probably some in your area already. If there aren't then consider making a page — people will find you. Otherwise you can turn your search to the depths of the Internet. There are numerous networks for ghost hunters on the Internet and our favorite resource is **PARANORMALSOCIETIES.COM**. This website can be a great reference.

2. Get comfortable saying no.

The world of ghost hunting tends to collect characters of all stripes. You'll find people that legitimately have a screw loose. You'll also find some of the most intelligent and empathetic people around. When you go on a ghost hunt you are opening yourself up to both the spirits in the room and the people around you. In short, you need to be comfortable with the people around you in order to have success. If you don't click with an individual then neither person should feel obliged to continue hunting with them.

3. Avoid the drama.

Some ghost hunters act like they are the main characters in some SyFy Network television show. They'll always have a story, always have an experience, and always seem able to one up you while on an investigation. While we are loathe to call people liars, especially in this field, you still have to be careful with whom you investigate. In a field that requires sincerity and humility, attaching yourself to a dramatically inclined individual can be a waste of time. You'll quickly learn to tell the difference between thrill seekers and legitimate ghost hunters.

4. Set your limits.

When you go ghost hunting you have to set your boundaries and know your limits. When you go ghost hunting with a partner you have to make sure that *they* know your limits. If you aren't comfortable sitting alone in a dark, dank basement then your partner needs to understand. Furthermore, some individuals will be attracted to chasing dark spirits by using controversial techniques (Ouija Boards, Provocation, Demon

Luring) and we suggest avoiding them. Real life isn't the movies, and real life ghost hunting is not something to be reckless with.

5. Identify strengths/weaknesses.

Everybody in life is different and as such we all have our own strengths and weaknesses. Consider crafting your ghost hunting team like you would a football or basketball team. I realized early on that I was great at staying calm, cool and focused. However, I'm naturally an emotionally closed off person. I had a friend who was interested in ghost hunting and he was *very* emotionally open. He was an empathetic person and I knew right away that he would be a great vessel during EVP sessions. So I invited him along and guided him through our hunts. He was able to pull in some great captures that I'm not positive I would have been able to acquire.

6. Enjoy yourself.

Finally you want to make sure that your ghost hunting team is enjoying themselves. Unless you are getting paid your focus should be on creating an experience that is positive and beneficial for everyone involved. Ghost hunting can be a thrilling adventure but it should also be an experience that you want to continually seek out. If you work with someone who is overbearing, ignorant, or rude then you will likely see negative results. While your focus is evidence first, your secondary focus should be to craft an enjoyable experience.

CHAPTER FIVE

CONDUCTING YOUR FIRST GHOST HUNT.

The biggest step in a ghost hunters life is their first big investigation. Now, you've probably already sat around your house with your EVP audio monitors. You might even have sat in on another investigation with a different crew. Now, however, we are going to talk about putting together our own investigation. I'll tell you a little bit about my first investigation and then we'll jump into laying out the basics for your first investigation.

Don't Make My Mistakes.

After capturing my first ever EVP I decided to throw myself wholesale into the world of ghost investigating. I had an insatiable desire to grab all of the gear that I could find, a few willing friends, and a potentially haunted location to go to. I didn't really think things through all of the way and as a result I hurt myself in the process.

My first full fledged investigation was in the **Schiller Piano Factory** which is located in Oregon, IL. The building was constructed in the late 1890s and it was a functioning piano for a number of years. The reason I chose this location was simple: I was from the area, I knew the owner, and I knew I could get in without any trouble. How often are you going to find a hook up as good as that? It was a giant three storied building with a history that I could stumble through — all for free. So what did I do wrong?

Well, to start out I definitely approached the building the wrong way. I felt that I was familiar with the area and the building so I didn't need to do any research. This is one of the cardinal sins of ghost hunting: **know your location**. Knowing the history of a location can guide you to asking the right sort of questions to instigate spiritual activity. In regards to **Schiller**, all I knew was that it used to be a piano factory. I had no idea that there had been a devastating fire on the first floor of the building nearly 50 years ago. Wouldn't I have gone there if I had known? But I didn't. That wasn't the only mistake that I had made.

To continue on, I ended up limiting myself with the type of evidence that I could capture. I knew that I needed a digital audio recorder to capture EVP action but I didn't know *when* or *how often* to actually run the device. So, what I ended up doing was only running my digital recorder when I was sitting down for an EVP session. What's the problem? Well, I was at the factory for eight hours and I only ended up with about 30 minutes worth of audio on my digital recorder. You do the math. Nowadays I bring multiple audio recorders and I *always* leave one running. As I investigate I will speak into my constantly running monitor to make notes. If I come upon sudden activity with my EMF detector then I don't even have to waste time getting out my recorder, I can just jump straight into it.

Finally, I wasn't prepared for what I would find and what it meant to bring something home with you. I went into the proverbial lions den with a nice juicy steak in my hands. What did I expect to happen? At the time I had little to no understanding in regards to demons or poltergeists. I was literally traveling with my spiritual eyes closed, unaware and uncaring of what I could find. Now that I know the dangers and risks associated with ghost hunting I can more capably prepare myself.

So, those are the big mistakes that I had made when I first started ghost hunting. Are you ready to plot out your first investigation? Let's dig deep and walk through all of the steps you'll need to follow in order to have a rock solid investigation.

Your First Hunt.

1. Find your location.

If you watch shows like *Paranormal Lockdown* or *Ghost Adventures* then you'll probably conclude that the only way to interact with spirits is by going to these elaborately haunted locations. It's true that certain buildings can be hubs for spiritual activity but that doesn't mean you can't think small. Look for an older building near you. Research the history of it. If anything catches your eye then add the building to your list of possibilities. You don't have to have deaths in a building for it to have spiritual activity. The world is old and people have traipsed around everywhere, leaving behind their energy imprints.

2. Evaluate your needs.

Let's say that you are investigating a condemned three story house with a limestone basement. What are you going to need for this investigation? Well, for starters you are going to want to evaluate the time of year that you are hunting. Is it cold out? Does the building have heat? Bring jackets, gloves, and hats in order to stay warm — let the spirits give you the chills. Next up you can start to lay out the building in your mind.

How many people will be investigating? How many cameras do you need? Do you have extra audio recorders for everyone? Having your team fully equipped at the start of the investigation is the best thing that you can do for your hunt. Being able to send individuals to different areas for solo investigations is an amazing feeling.

3. Decide your approach.

The most exciting portion of any ghost investigation occurs when the lights are off and your plan is being put into place. When I investigated the Ashmore Estates I wanted to make sure that I gave myself the opportunity to seek out specific spirits. The Ashmore Estates had been a home for the mentally ill and the physically infirm. There was a sweet little girl that lived in the house and she tragically passed away due to a fire. I had heard rumblings that she was still in the building and my goal for the night was to communicate with her and bring her some peace or enjoyment. So I brought a toy for her to play with. Whenever I was seeking out the child I was careful in regards to my tone, the words I used, and my general demeanor. I wanted to be inviting, not intimidating. My approach going into Ashmore was to be a calming presence for this child. Now look at the building that you plan on investigating — decide your approach.

4. Hit your marks.

The worst thing in the world is finishing an investigation and coming to the realization that you didn't capture enough audio or video to analyze at a later time. Before going into your investigation make a check list of all the rooms you want to investigate and all of the techniques that you want to employ. Reference my chapter on 'Ghost Hunting Techniques' and utilize them where appropriate. Have multiple people try each technique to see if you get different results. The more information that you gather, the more likely it is that you will actually capture something of note.

5. Be patient during your hunt.

We currently live in a world of instant gratification and this leads us to becoming bored or disinterested at an alarming rate. When it comes to ghost investigation you have to realize that the majority of your time will be spent sitting in silence, in the dark. Of course you should still be enjoying yourself, but this is not the quick paced action that the television shows would lead you to believe. There are literally handfuls of hours being cut from the episodes. You are seeing the highlights of what likely was a 10 or 12 hour investigation. Don't lose hope. Accept it as part of the process and learn to embrace it.

6. Analyze your findings.

The actual investigation is only the beginning of your work. When you conclude your investigation you should be leaving with hours of video recordings, hours of audio recordings, and even a couple folders full of photographs. While this is a tall and intimidating task, it is nor your job to go through all of your data to find any traces of spirit activity. Grab a nice pair of headphones and upload the files into your computer. Sit back and listen through each individual file while marking down on a timesheet any potential findings. You'll be *shocked* by what you find. Don't feel obligated to go through it all at once. You can even delegate some of the files to other members of your team.

One of my personal favorite pieces of evidence occurred when I was scrubbing through audio of my friend and I just talking in between EVP sessions. We had gotten sidetracked and were discussing a different room when a voice clearly, and loudly, appeared on the file: "Chrissss." Clear as day, and loud, this voice hissed out the name of my investigative partner. I almost fell out of my chair when I replayed the audio. This is what's called a Class A EVP — clear, cut and dry.

A Final Note.

No two investigations will ever be the same because no two spirits will ever be alike. Spirits are people or, more accurately, *were* people. You never know what you are going to find. Some spirits are happy to engage you. Others are surly and annoyed by your intrusion on their life. Some are sad and some are even dangerous. The best thing you can do is go in with a clear cut plan of attack. When you are prepared you are ready for everything.

CLOSING THOUGHTS

So, you've made it to the end. Congratulations. You've read all of the information that I wished I had read before my first investigation. You are dipping your toes into a whole new world, literally, and what you are likely to find can be invigorating and terrifying. While this book contains enough information to get you started, it still isn't telling you everything. The best thing that you can do is approach each investigation as if it were a test and then study appropriately for it.

If this was your first foray into the spiritual realm then you likely are having trouble digesting what you just learned. Once you interact with your first spirit your life is going to change — forever. I know that my life changed dramatically after my first experience. The fact that I was recording when I had my experience is only a benefit: I can relive the moment over and over again. Conceptually you are going to have to wrestle with the concept of life after death. You are going to have to try and find a way for spirits to coexist with whatever world view you might hold. Most of all you are now going to need to keep a level head.

Now would be a great time to reach out and try to connect with other paranormal inclined individuals in order to share your newfound interest. Coming to the realization that the paranormal world *is* real can be a heady thing. Having someone to bounce your thoughts, new evidence, and theories off of can create a comfortable environment. Head to the message boards, go to the chatrooms, pay attention to local bulletin boards. You'll find other people like you out there.

Lastly, if you enjoyed this book or found it useful **at all** I would appreciate a review left on my page. My goal is to put information out there that can be helpful to aspiring paranormal investigators. Your words of support mean the world.

Happy Hunting,

Randall.

Made in the USA
Monee, IL
16 December 2022

21877783R00020